Tap Dancing

for the Relatives

Tap Dancing

for the Relatives

Poems by
Richard Michelson

Illustrations by Barry Moser

University Presses of Florida

University of Central Florida Press
Orlando

University Presses of Florida, the agency of the State of Florida's university system for publication of scholarly and creative works, operates under policies adopted by the Board of Regents. Its offices are located at 15 Northwest 15th Street, Gainesville, Florida 32603.

Library of Congress information appears at the end of the book.

In memory of my father
            who entrusted his stories
and for my mother
            who loaned me the words

Acknowledgments

Some of these poems originally appeared in the following publications: *Poetry Northwest, Southern Poetry Review, Mid-American Review, Jewish Currents, Bellingham Review, Pikestaff Review, Oyez Review, Salome, Beyond Baroque, Small Pond Magazine of Literature,* and *Matrix.*

"Where I Sat" was reprinted in *The Anthology of Magazine Verse: Yearbook of American Poetry.*

Eleven of these poems originally appeared in a limited edition chapbook, *The Head of the Family,* published by the Red Herring Press.

Contents

I. Dancing above Brooklyn Heights

II. Dancing with My Arms in the Air

III. Dancing Our Hearts Out

Words then, hurt worse than stones.
It was so with the ancient Hebrews:
a curse could kill,
a prayer part seas.
Words carefully chosen
had the importance of blood.
But that, like I said,
was before your time.
I was still a boy.

Samuel Jochnowitz, 1890–1973

I

Dancing above

Brooklyn Heights

A BIRTHDAY CARD FROM MY FATHER

I.

When we visit the old neighborhood
people tell my father he is looking good;
they think he is *his* father,
dead some twenty years.
It is tradition in our family:
the men age quickly
but marry women with youthful eyes.

It makes for complications.
I won't lie. At my wedding
the Rabbi called my mother
by her maiden name,
said she wasn't Mrs. Michelson, yet.
Be patient.

My father laughs.
He knows there are advantages too.
People see a face like mine,
a girl like this,
they think I must be rich
or else a giant in bed.
Either way they treat me with importance.

II.

On vacation, my father films road signs
to prove where he has been.
A beach he might forget. Bahama? Bermuda?
A fountain in France can cry as well in Italy.
Who can remember such things?
But years are more important.
He shouts his out
like numbers in a Jewish bakery
on Sunday mornings.

I never understood my father's love for birthdays.
How bad could he need a new tie?
It must be something else he wrapped
around his neck each June,
one hand conducting the New York Philharmonic,
the other sliding between my mother's breasts.

III.

Father, today on my birthday
I walked alone past your house.
The rhythmic drip of years,
that chinese torture,
followed me even there.
I ran from your yard like a boy believing
his last inch of dry clothing
would protect him from the storm.

I should have stayed.
I'd have seen a man kick up his heels
like Gene Kelly in the rain.
We could have tap-danced toward the mailbox
arm in arm; two beats of a single heart.
The point is, father, I thank you for your card.

A DOCTOR OF PAINT AND HARDWARE

Rolling down the car windows
in ninety degrees of heat
you could be my grandfather
rolling out the patched awning
for another day's work.
You must learn the look of success.
Even the poor no longer trust doctors
without air conditioning
and electric windows.
Already you are suspect
for making the housecalls
that were so much a part of
my grandfather's business,
my grandfather's time.
A doctor of paint and hardware
is what he called himself,
and each day between three and four
he closed the shop and pushed
a homemade wooden cart
with oversized iron wheels
through the streets. "Business?"
he would say, "I can't complain."
These days people offer good money
for iron wheels. They lean them
against posts in front of their houses
as if to say: "And see what a success

I have become." My grandfather
would not have understood.
He sweated fifteen years
to buy father a used Ford
and then made him park it
behind a neighbor's yard.
People, he said, would never believe
that an honest man
could afford such a car.

THE WILDEST OF SISTERS

I.

At his own wedding
Lew danced through lunch.
He said "Kosher means kosher.
Why take chances?"
Even today he'll hide behind the refrigerator
to catch Aunt Dot shelling oysters.
It's twenty years since she cared.

II.

When my father was eleven
he wore Trojans to his morning prayers.
This is his favorite story:
"So the Rabbi says phylactories—
so I hear prophylactics."
Uncle Lew begins to choke. My father's laugh
sticks in his throat like a pearl.

III.

You don't tell Uncle Lew about the streets.
He knows the score.

"For two years who kept Brooklyn clean?
Me! Lewis. A penny per bottle
I bought my first car.
Don't cry to me
about the poor."

IV.

On my birthday
Aunt Dot slips me ten.
It is a secret passing between us.
She calls it funding for the arts.
"I wrote poetry myself," she says
"when I was your age, maybe younger."

V.

Their first daughter was born retarded.
"A toss of the dice," the doctor said.
Lew prefers to talk of other things.
Here is a photo of him and Aunt Dot
the eve of their wedding.
Lew never looked finer. His right hand
holds his supper like a sack of gold.
His left hand rests on Aunt Dot's knee.
It is hard to imagine her growing up
as the wildest of sisters
but my mother assures me it was so.

MY MOTHER'S FAMILY
GROWS SMALLER

with each wedding
until only four chairs remain. Tonight,
remembering the time of six tables, her eyes
dance around the hall, fall upon Aunt Debbie
dancing the Nagilah; Uncle Bob's breath, short,
tagging behind like a younger brother's,
will within the year overtake his wife's
cancer-filled body. Aunt Dot bunny hops,
hop, hop, hop, her hands gloved with sweat
grasp Uncle Lew's waist the secret way
she'll hold him late that night, listening
to the tap of strange footsteps
climbing their basement stairs.
Retired to Florida, Uncle Phil completes
Shubert's "unfinished" and angles
his lawn chair away from the town.
My mother's family grows smaller
with each phone call, each uneasy silence.
But today is for long shots.
She leads us in a hokey-pokey:
Uncle Bob, Uncle Lew, my wife and I.
We circle our chairs and laugh so loudly
that no can hear when the music dies down.

AUNT FRIEDA ABOVE
BROOKLYN HEIGHTS

On this street
there's nothing to hold onto—
a man or a value—
and so it isn't funny
the way Aunt Frieda
on her way to the grocery
found herself dancing
above Brooklyn Heights
like a dollar bill
caught in the wind.
Nobody even looked up
she told us later
and each shake of her head
lifted her that much higher
until she refused
to even step outside
without filling her pockets
with pennies
and just enough troubles
to weigh her down.

AUNT FRIEDA IN THE MOVIES

In the moving pictures
Aunt Frieda is the one
standing stone still. We dance
around her; my sister making faces
Mom says will freeze on her face
until no man will want her;
me leaping from behind
screaming "bugga, bugga, bugga!"

No use.

She will not budge.
Not until the lights go out
and the camera is tucked quietly
back in its case
does Aunt Frieda turn and slowly
begin to move.

AUNT FRIEDA WATCHES THE CLOCK

Aunt Frieda watches the clock
remembers
to remind Mother that it's time
I washed for bed. Dad whistles
from the washroom, one short note
that means: no nonsense, listen
to your aunt, she can't remember
if you're eight or nine this year
or home from college with a lover
who isn't Jewish, God forbid, but
since when was Ruth the Moab;
so climb the stairs and give your family
some little pleasure; let Aunt Frieda
pat your tuchis "tataleh, gay schlafen!"

And tomorrow we'll discuss that other matter.

AUNT FRIEDA'S BLUFF

Like mismatched luggage, Aunt Frieda's last teeth lean
against each other, rising above her lower lip
like a skyline of low-rent apartments. Her heart attacks
like a neighbor's poodle, nips at her ankles, each step
a small pain. Half-blind, she welcomes me by my sister's
name, waves Mother goodbye, not to worry.
But Sister and I, our heads hanging low
as Aunt Frieda's breasts, hear Dad packing her bags
in the back of the Packard while Aunt Frieda peeks
through the venetian blinds.

AUNT FRIEDA IN THE OLD-AGE HOME

Even here she looks old.
She is not really my aunt
but my mother's aunt.
Maybe her mother's.
No one remembers.
She never dated
and mother doubts
she'd have married
had she been asked.
There was enough on her mind.
For one, she was growing old.
Older than she weighed
with her shoes on.

I visit because
no one else does.
When I die, Frieda says
she'll have no one.

A GRANDMOTHER'S ADVICE

Dear Rick,

    Your poems lately are too well done.
Lines stuffed tighter than my turkeys,
bulge like your too tight blue swimsuit.
A show-off just like your father.
    Your mother informs me you still see
that shiksa with the mouth
where her manners should be.
    With me it's okay
but grandfather has been ill.
When I read him your poems he lowers
his head as though avoiding stones,
so great is his faith in the word.
He says he should suffer long enough
to hear you speak from the heart.
Come visit Pesach.
We are too long apart.

            All my love,
            Gramma

FIFTY DOLLARS

I.

"In Hebrew your name is Sol,"
my mother said,
"in whose memory
Aunt Dee deposits
each year
fifty dollars
toward your account."

Fifty dollars. Fifty dollars
would last me fifteen Chanukahs,
five thousand sweeps
of my father's store.
I could retire,
hand back my broom.
I'm talking here
not only fifty dollars
but fifty dollars a year.

II.

What will I say
when my son asks
about Uncle Sol?

He was my mother's only brother
and he lived for eighteen years.
I had imagined him in battle
strong as General Grant
posing for the fifty dollar bill
but lately he has shaved his fine beard
and taken on the earlocks
of a cheder boy.

In grandmother's house,
still heavy with the weight
of fifty years
of family photographs
I search alone for Uncle Sol.
He hides behind long-forgotten
friends of my father,
penciling his name
beneath every man
my mother never knew.

WHEN I WAS YOUR AGE

the tubes of light in the cathedral
radio were Camels puffed by the Bowery Boys
between their lines. But even they knew the th-thump
of father's heavy boot in the stairwell
and they'd snuff out their butts
while I high-tailed mine into bed.
Now I know that that radio stayed hot
enough to fry eggs for breakfast, and I suspect
father saw the last crack of light
scramble out from under our front door.
But when I was your age, snoring
like a short-wave station, as the broom
of his lip swept me into darker dreams,
I thought only (as you do now) of how
The Boys and I had outwitted, once again,
our father's leather hand.

DOWN ON ONE KNEE
HE'S A NATURAL

Down on one knee he's a natural
Jolson, Rizzuto at shortstop, Casey crouched
for the killshot, coaxing "Come to papa."
My first step was a Spaulding dizzy
with english, pink and spinning,
little wounded warbler. An inch off
the floor, his right arm flashes, a snap
of the wrist. He taught me to stare
straight into the camera, to stand
front and center and never show fear.

Down on one knee he proposed to my mother,
danced with my sister, and wrestled
with me. Down on both knees his body
attacks him like a dog attacks its tail, turns
him in circles. This picture I cannot forget:
It takes all his great strength just to breathe.

SHOES

Pride parades up my ankles, struts
on spiked heels and steel-hardened toes.
Shitkickers they were called;
safe passage through the streets;
shined by small boys and spit
they marched me everywhere but home.
There my father called them cockroach killers
and cuffed the side of my head.
He said if there's any kicking to do
it's between his shoe and my sweet ass.
He said two things he wouldn't stand for
were streetfights and poems.

II.

Hushpuppies, wingtips, blue suedes
line the foot of his bed. Friends
file past: pennyloafers, high heels,
little galoushes with his runny nose.
Father, the more pages turned
the more I learn to distrust words.
I slip into pipe and slippers,
walk nearer to the ground.
If my soul doesn't burn
I'll follow barefoot into heaven.

TAP DANCING FOR THE RELATIVES

Eight and alone at last, I'm old
enough to care for myself, to stand
behind the bedroom door and hold it
closed. Already my hand
moves me like a woman's and
the moon's light taps against the window.

My father warned that children who cry out
in their dreams and fear the dark, die
in their sleep. I stayed awake each night
that week until my mother tucked me
into bed. Young boys don't die so easily;
you have to suffer first, she said.

The nightlight is so thick with life,
the moths can barely flap their wings.
They don't complain, although light only brings
them death. They'd rather live
briefly, I think, than have to sing
and tap-dance for the relatives.

II

Dancing with My Arms

in the Air

A MODEL FOR MARRIAGE

I.

I have this model I walk through
like those new suburban homes
on corner lots. Always open,
with guides to watch my step.
In this kitchen my mother learned
to love to cook. I mean that
sincerely. My father loved to eat.
You need to know more? Here
in the bathroom, my father sat
each Sunday reading *War and Peace*.
"If you have to go, go
on Saturday. Your father works
hard all week."
You want to see the bedroom?
Take my word.
They are very much in love.

II.

When we married
my mother sent us matching underwear
tagged "Made in heaven." My father
turned all of a sudden

serious
and kissed us both.
"The perfect pair," he said,
"A model marriage!"
You should have heard the fuss
when you left.

III.

You write now about success,
a career, a trail of guilt
longer than any wedding train.
A marriage is no small thing.
Here on Sundays I sit
and read your letters.
Our problem is love.
Take my word. Our problem
is that love is not our problem.
I walk through this house sick
of my own encouragements
that keep you far from me.
"What could be so important?"
is perched like the song of a bird
on my mother's lips.

FROM THE BENCH

My mother bats dishrags on the fifth-story sill.
Her wrists snap and bread crumbs swirl like light rain
over right field, where, between Finestein's Deli
and Shelly's Fish Market, my father inches in, shuffling
both feet; he tugs at his crotch and shrugs
his left shoulder. Imagine his grin

like a Hank Aaron home run, fading from view,
his teeth dark as pennies as he pedals back,
his back to the street where six days a week
he wields the same hammer, pounding Sabbath nearer.

I cheer from the bench, the chalk-marked curb
that defines our neighborhood. It's my job to rattle
the opposing pitcher, and I intend to shake him up
good; to make him anxious as mother was when father,
down the alley, disappeared like a dream of a high
hanging slider, like the first girl I disappointed

in bed. She swiveled her hips while I turned on
the TV in time to watch Mays beat the Mets
with a double that bounced by Swoboda
and into the stands. It was father, I swear,

who held up that baseball high over his head
and saluted the crowd. I imagine he stood till the last

fan had left before returning home to the woman
who cooked his three meals a day, forty years
and then slept, not caring to hear why at times
men perform like boys squirming on benches.

SCHENCK STREET NEAR PITKIN

We walk past other people's houses. I peek into their
    lives
and see the shapes of childhood friends, the weight
they've taken on like the pounds a mother gains
and passes down to her children. My wife pouts at the
    stars

uncertain where good manners end and argument is
    proper.
She would escape this foolishness of mine
but cannot walk a South Side street alone
she tells and tells me; until I slow the pace to prove

a man's advantage, and stop beneath a window
    promising
some small voyeur's reward. A woman unbuttons her
    blouse,
faces her lover, then pulls the shade.
He'll fill her emptiness a thousandth time

with dreams of London, Porto Bello, Paris. Is he the man
I'd have become if I still lived near Pitkin?
I turn to touch my wife who will be sleeping
by the time I recognize this house and enter.

WIFEBEATING

There's not a mark on her body.
I've learned from my father's mistakes.
The back of his hand to the side of my face
brought back notes from the teacher,
a buzzing that lingered for days.
Mother's sting was less direct.
She'd poke a word under my skin;
I never even noticed until it began to ache.
She learned from grandfather's mistakes.
He'd lindy like a caged bear, shake
imagined bars, rage darkening his eyes.
Listen. Only beginners leave scars.
I've learned from my mother's tears.
My words float downwards, circle
calmly like a long joke lost
in the telling. Who would suspect?
Tonight I am in control.
I dance with my arms in the air.

READING THE ADVICE COLUMNS

Today, a bad day for Ann.
Another hard-working family man
died suddenly, and his wife, signed UNSURE
IN CHICAGO, found love poems in his dresser drawer.

Today Ann is mad at all men.
How many times must she warn?
Mister—Keep your underwear clean.
Women at least you can train.

My wife, as a child, learned to fear
embarrassment and mistrust her luck.
She says Ann says tidy your affairs.
No one means to be hit by God's truck.

II.

Before mother read the columns
she'd remove the scissors from her sewing box,
spread out the patient on the kitchen table
and limber up her fingers. She'd slip clippings
in my books and my lunchbox.
DISOBEDIENT CHILD. I'd find Abby
dripping with cream cheese and lox.

III.

Father read them on the sly. He'd hide
a column in with the headlines and look
both ways. Caught one day reading *Playboy*,
to mother's complaints, he repeated
what Abby had dared to write. Who cares
where he works up an appetite,
as long as he comes
home to eat.

IV.

Today, a good day for Ann.
She saved EIGHTH GRADE AND UNSURE
from going too far. Ann accepts
her thanks on behalf of us all.

I look up at my wife, our month-old daughter
and feel foolish for feeling safer.
Rereading the letter out loud
I recognize my mother's voice.

Some evenings we'd guess at Ann's answers
and call out our own and we'd argue
all night till our own voices woke us.
It was, many times, the only time we spoke.

FOR MISS B., MY EIGHTH-GRADE ENGLISH TEACHER WHO ASKED: "HOW DO YOU EXPECT TO WRITE POETRY WHEN YOU DON'T EVEN KNOW HOW TO BEHAVE?!"

Answers come to me still.
Sometimes, driving through dreams
I spit them out rapidfire
and sharp as tacks
on rainslick pavement.
You wave me down, screaming
I don't know how to behave.

What did you expect?
It was a difficult grade
for us both. I, two years
till my first lover,
you since your last.
Sometimes I think of you naked
and needing the extra credits.
I have to beg you to behave.

How things turn out!
I read *Silas Marner* after all,
and majored in English,

and wrote you this poem, you
who would flip back my head
like, you said, "a pez dispenser
full of wisecracks." A weak
simile. Still, come to me:

After twenty years
it's time we forgave
I offer you this.
I don't know how else to behave.

LIKE TALK

I've seen enough movies to know
that no one ever had a Pullman this small.
The shade, up, allows us both an extra breath.
Our knees, careful dancers, brush and bump.
This train to Milano. Fifteen hours across
from each other, uncomfortable as parents
whose last child has left home. "So," you say,
"we may as well talk." From my seat
I already see the Alps in the distance.

In every station there are women I could love.
I choose a mademoiselle, her features foreign,
but suddenly familiar as yours. "In Italy"
you tell me, "the men stare directly at you."
Reflected in my window, the outline of your eyes
frames young Bogart kissing his sweetheart goodbye.

Nothing is crueler than a train on time.
Its whistle mocks the last pleas of those crowding
the platform. A man taps at our window, too dark
to see in through. He orders his children
to stop fighting, or some uncle, with chocolates,
will not meet them at the border.
I want to tell our momentary father
not to worry; that a comfortable silence,
like talk, has settled upon us.

THE ORGY

I am a bridegroom again,
melting under the gaze of in-laws.
I mumble some name, perhaps my own.
I will not answer for my intentions.

In every mirror another shadow
is slipping off your shoes,
stripping off the months of silence
that have settled upon us.

I light the fire and its flames surround us.
Wanting you from every angle,
my eyes leap from woman to woman,
loving each in her turn.

You step forward and turn
your thousand eyes toward me.
I slide with the lace down your thighs.
We ride on the ribs of the floor.

How far we have traveled to tend to
our marriage in this paradise

of mirrors, this single room
with no room to hide.

I watch as the couple above us curve
together like question marks.
His chest fits snug to her back.
The embers tap-dance in the dark.

III

Dancing Our Hearts Out

THE JEWS THAT WE ARE

> . . . you have inherited its burden
> without its misery.
> Elie Wiesel

I.

March 1979 and I am watching Nazis
march through Chicago. The bold type
of the *Sun-Times* describes a small band
of hoodlums, undereducated boyscouts, the better
to be ignored. My grandfather, back
hunched over his Bible, agrees. Jews like myself
should stay home, should lay down
our stones and pray like the Jews that we are.

II.

Grandfather, you are easy to love
with your long beard and the way you sway
like a palm branch in the storm. It is easy
to romanticize your spiritual search,
worldly naiveté and wise rabbinical words.
You belong in the books I read
by Singer, Peretz, Sholom Aleichem.
But their characters are ignorant
of the chapters to come. You know
where their prayers will lead.

III.

A circle. Six Nazis. Full military garb.
Your daughter naked in the middle. A gang-
rape and you're more ashamed than angry.
One soldier says all Jewesses are whores
and the others agree. You say nothing.
Years later you'll decide to speak:
"Do we not serve Hitler's purpose, we
who would sooner renounce our beliefs
than assume our burdens?" My mother
turns aside. Afraid
to answer. Silent even in her dreams.

IV.

A generation after the Holocaust
and I know no Hebrew, no Torah. I fast
only on the day of atonement
and even then I've been known to cheat.
A generation after the Holocaust
and I apologize for my grandfather's
bent back and wild gestures.
I used to tremble to the discordant
rhythm of his prayers. I feared the mysterious
words that kept us from the devil.
Next to me my mother slept. She never cried
out in her dreams for his protection.
From her window she watches Nazis

march. Their feet strike the pavement
like the constant ticking of a clock.
I am a Jew a generation after the Holocaust.
Poorer, my grandfather says, without a past,
than he, who has no future.

THE NEED TO DANCE

I.

I hear them each night
like a shy shuffling of feet
on the dance floor. A charity ball
in the Great Hall closet.
My mind, clouded with sleep
and years of Russian novels,
easily imagines gray-whiskered gentlemen
waltzing past tables of wine and cheese.
In the corner I sit with my grandfather.
He talks me back to bed
with witching tales of Lutsk
and the women of Vienna.

II.

My mother's eyes are burning.
Tension snaps them shut
like an oven door. Trapped
in one dream for years she knows
a Jewish girl learned to dance
or stood against the wall.
Someone calls for a polka
and she's tossed with her pillow
from partner to partner
like any two-dollar whore.

III.

My grandfather, too, died dancing.
From the start he started out on the wrong foot.
"People are people,"
he'd say over and over,
curling his lip like a Solomon,
"what they need is to laugh and to dance."
And his toes would tap
and his bones begin to rattle like a beggar's cup.
And such good that it did.
Before he died they sat in a circle,
clapped out a two-step
and laughed as he danced his heart out.

GENUINE JEWISH FLESH

I.

Rabbi Abe Rosen returned
home from Hell pulls from his pocket
a cake of soap. Says, "Hope"
from his pulpit "stinks
like an armpit. Its smell
must be always upon you."

II.

White, she was, as mayonnaise on white bread
when Abe's smooth-cheeked son cut his strings
and tied himself a tight goyisha knot.
"Milk" he said, "flows like life through her veins."
But then he sucked at her breast
and blood spilled like wine from a broken jar.
Never sleep with a Jew during times of war.

III.

These things did happen
                    confessed the chaplain
who blessed the knife
                    that butchered Abe's wife.
This is the vat
                    where they boiled her fat
until it was soap.
                    This is the soap.

IV.

Rabbi Abe Rosen   returned
home to Heaven   pulls from his pocket
a cake of soap.   Says, "Hope"
from his coffin   "hangs loose
like a foreskin.   Its weight
serves no purpose   to speak of."

WHERE I SAT

I sat between Grandmother
and Aunt Etta.
I never had a chance.

Grandmother would point to
her forearm, the numbers
tattooed there and that's
how I learned to count.
Aunt Etta told lies about
men who had loved her
when she was a young
coquette. I sat

like the silence
between train whistles
and dreamt

of the first woman
that took me to bed.
She was so beautiful
I never had a chance;
her skin
as smooth

as her silence. I heard
bells and sat

like a boy mid-bath,
between curiosity
and my own nakedness.

I sat between Grandmother
and Aunt Etta.
Between spoonfuls
of regret
they fed me
from this you shouldn't know
and may you never forget.

THE OLD SPEAK YIDDISH

The old speak Yiddish
Great Grandma   Great Grandad
Under their breath
Aunt Frieda   Aunt Becky
As if they've misplaced their teeth
Or forgotton why they've phoned
Or the reasons they've suffered

Their children speak Yiddish
Mother   and Father
Inside their houses
Aunt Rae   Uncle Nathan
As if they know some secret
We'll learn when we're older
In the street they speak English

The young teach English
Cousin Bev   Cousin Isa
In schools   In the Office
Cousin Larry   Cousin Lenny
Talk law or talk money
And the old are engaged
To look after their children

Their children learn Hebrew
Eddie   Alissa

Once each week at the temple
Sanford   Camie and Esther
And they think all old people
Begin to speak Yiddish
Under their breath

So that death shouldn't hear them

JERUSALEM

I. The Flight

We circle. We circle
until Grandfather's dizzy,
his head spinning like the glass globe
on which he'd measure, in inches,
the distance from America. As he prayed,
blood would pulse through his veins,
his forehead mapping the traditional
borders of Israel. Leaning
toward the window I can see
no farther than the fear reflected
in the dark clouds under his eyes.
It tells me that we are circling
and this is no time for uncertainty.
I watch a prayer dance
down my grandfather's throat.
The clouds dissolve. I think
I can see Jerusalem.

II. The Walled City

These catwalks weave
like so many false messiahs
through the Walled City.

The paths turn, reconsider,
circle back. Beneath the weight
of an eight-foot wooden cross
men pose their wives. All along
the Via Dolorosa, women wave
as Grandfather walks
straight toward the Wailing Wall.

III. The Temple Mount

Here, where even stones are symbols
and to stumble on a tree root
becomes the surest sign; somewhere
near the Holiest of Holies
my eyes turn from the rock
where Abraham kissed Isaac,
and all belief and holy men are left behind.
Here, where Grandfather fears to step,
I sightsee down the paths his prayers
have carved through history, while he
waits on the sidestreet, where,
like Moses, all old men shake
at the edge of their dreams.

IV. The Mount of Olives

One does not visit the Mount of Olives
to escape the smell of death.
I have many questions
to ask of Grandfather

but he is both silent
and sad. When the Messiah calls
these first lucky few to Heaven,
he will be burrowing underground
from his grave in New York,
certain that Heaven is
an overbooked airflight
with just so many seats.

MY GRANDFATHER'S SHIRT

I button my grandfather's shirt
The skin he had shed at his death
That covers me now by his will

The wind blows a thought to my brain
A thought that was his and not mine
I pray to his god this one time

My obstinance formed in his image
Hard years we had passed without speaking
Silence harder on him than a boy

An old man he was when he called me
Full of fear to his hospital side
To pray that I pray that one time

I turned as he called for my heart
To turn my eyes in toward the soul
Till I turn toward belief in his will

Two men having only in common
The tears held back deep in their heads
One watching one fade into image

I hold for all time in this pocket
A thought that was his and not mine
And I pray as I button his shirt
That he might hear my voice this one time

THE HEAD OF THE FAMILY

I.

You never did get used to the suit and tie.
You would tug at your sleeves
till they rolled like window shades
up to your elbows,
unbutton the collar.
A deck of cards could relax in your hands.
Still this was a formal portrait,
the only image you ever allowed.
Perhaps you already knew that your wife was dying
and you wanted us to remember her
by your side.
You seem proud.
It's the hat that does it.
You knew how to wear a hat.
You could have given Bogey lessons,
taught Sinatra the perfect tilt.
To you it came natural.
There never was even one mirror
around the house.

II.

The dress might have been chosen
to blend into the background brick and trees,
but the lines in her face will not let her recede.

She is no longer the shy girl
hiding behind the handsome gambler.
You are not bluffing for books and shoes.
When you turned toward God
she didn't expect an explanation.
She learned to keep a kosher house
become a seamstress
and finished raising the five children
with little help.
Through it all she never even changed expressions.
There must have been something
she wanted to say.

III.

You were the head of the family.
I'd heard stories.
But what was I to think
seeing you confined to your chair,
reading Torah day and night, your hat
replaced by a plain black yarmulke,
your hands grown thin and brittle as matzos.
Still, I'd heard stories
so what was I to do, a boy of twelve,
but sneak into your room?
Deep in the dust of your closet
I found that old hat
and placed it like a crown
upon my head.
Like your death, it fell
in front of my eyes.

Richard Michelson was born in Brooklyn, New York, and grew up there and on Long Island. He holds degrees from SUNY–Albany and Goddard College.

His poems and essays have appeared in many of the country's most prominent literary journals. He owns art galleries in Amherst, Massachusetts, where he lives with his wife, Jennifer, and their two children, and in Northampton.

Library of Congress Cataloging-in-Publication Data

Michelson, Richard.
    Tap dancing for the relatives.

    (University of Central Florida contemporary poetry
series)
        I. Title. II. Series.
PS3563.I4T3 1985   811'.54   85–9166
ISBN 0–8130–0827–1 (alk. paper)

UNIVERSITY OF CENTRAL FLORIDA
Contemporary Poetry Series

George Bogin, *In a Surf of Strangers*
Van K. Brock, *The Hard Essential Landscape*
Gerald Duff, *Calling Collect*
Malcolm Glass, *Bone Love*
Susan Hartman, *Dumb Show*
Lola Haskins, *Planting the Children*
Hannah Kahn, *Time, Wait*
Michael McFee, *Plain Air*
Richard Michelson, *Tap Dancing for the Relatives*
David Posner, *The Sandpipers*
Nicholas Rinaldi, *We Have Lost Our Fathers*
CarolAnn Russell, *The Red Envelope*
Robert Siegel, *In a Pig's Eye*
Edmund Skellings, *Face Value*
Edmund Skellings, *Heart Attacks*